Readers

Owls

And Other Animals
With Amazing Eyes

by
Susan Labella

Children's Press®
A Division of Scholastic Inc.
New York Toronto London Auckland Sydney
Mexico City New Delhi Hong Kong
Danbury, Connecticut

These content vocabulary word builders
are for grades 1-2.

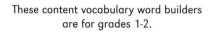

Consultant: Rodney B. Siegel
Research Scientist, The Institute for Bird Populations

Curriculum Specialist: Linda Bullock

Special thanks to Omaha's Henry Doorly Zoo

Photo Credits:

Photographs © 2005: Alan Sieradzki/Global Owl Project: 2, 4 bottom right, 8; Animals Animals/Zig Leszczynski: 4 bottom left, 15; Connie Toops: 5 bottom left, 10; Corbis Images: 23 top right (David Aubrey), back cover (Royalty-Free), 4 top, 19; Dembinsky Photo Assoc./Thomas Boyden: center cover inset, 23 top left (Darrell Gulin), 23 bottom right (Marilyn & Maris Kazmers), 11 (Jim Roetzel); Dwight R. Kuhn Photography: 20, 21; Minden Pictures/Tim Fitzharris: 1, 7; Nature Picture Library Ltd./Nick Gordon: 23 bottom left; Peter Arnold Inc.: top cover inset (Fred Bravendam), 5 top right, 9 (Sylvain Cordier); Photo Researchers, NY: 17 (Darwin Dale), cover background (E. R. Degginger), 5 bottom right, 5 top left, 13 (Martin Dohrn), 18 (Dr. Paul A. Zahl); Seapics.com/Masa Ushioda: bottom cover inset.

Book Design: Simonsays Design!

Library of Congress Cataloging-in-Publication Data

LaBella, Susan, 1948-
    Owls and other animals with amazing eyes / by Susan Labella.
       p. cm. — (Scholastic news nonfiction readers)
    Includes bibliographical references and index.
    ISBN 0-516-24927-4 (lib. bdg.)
    1. Eye—Juvenile literature. 2. Owls—Juvenile literature. I. Title. II. Series.
    QL949.L25 2005
    573.8'8—dc22
                                            2005003098

1 2 3 4 5 6 7 8 9 10 R 14 13 12 11 10 09 08 07 06 05

CONTENTS

WORD HUNT

Look for these words as you read. They will be in **bold**.

anableps
(**an**-uh-bleps)

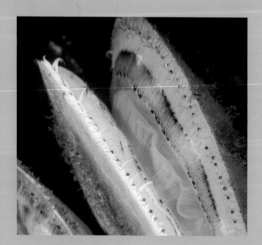

scallop
(**skal**-uhp)

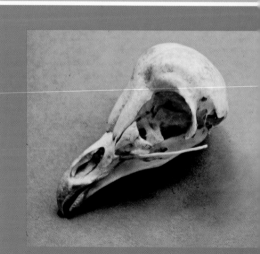

skull
(skuhl)

cricket
(**krik**-it)

owl
(oul)

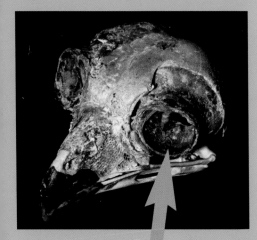

socket
(**sok**-it)

spider
(**spy**-dur)

Eyes! Eyes!

What's so amazing about animal eyes?

Some animals have eyes that can see well in the dark.

Other animals use their eyes to see underwater.

Let's look at how different animals use their eyes.

This is a great horned owl.
It can see well in the dark.

Some **owls** have eyes that fill about half of their **skull**.

The skull is the bony part of the owl's head.

skull

This barn owl has very big eyes.

An owl's eyes sit tight in their **sockets**.

The eyes don't move in the sockets.

Instead, owls spin their heads to look for food.

sockets

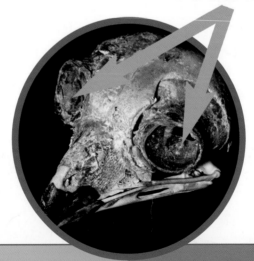

These are burrowing owls. Look! One owl is spinning its head.

A jumping **spider** has eight eyes to help it find food.

All eight eyes move up, down, back, and forth.

This helps the spider see insects to eat, like **crickets**.

cricket

This spider is jumping!
Will it catch the cricket?

A **scallop** has 100 eyes!

Its eyes can see shadows that pass by.

If an enemy comes near, the scallop swims away fast.

eyes

Look at all the eyes
on this scallop!

15

A bee can see color with its eyes.

This bee can find bright flowers that have nectar.

Nectar is juice from a flower.

A bee drinks nectar to make honey.

This fish's eyes can see above and below the water at the same time!

This fish is called an **anableps**.

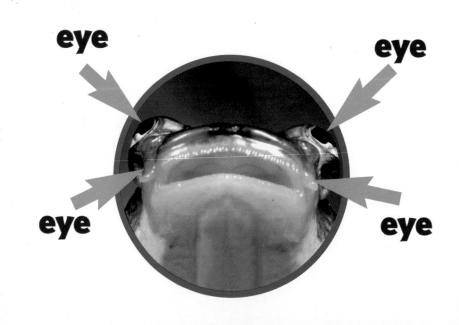

eye

eye

eye

eye

This fish catches its food from the air and from the water. Yum!

Owl Eyes Hunt!
How does a Saw-whet owl catch food?

1 This owl uses its big yellow eyes to find food at night.

2 It sees something! What can it be? The owl flies closer to see.

5

Time to eat!
The owl used its
eyes to help it
find dinner!

4

The owl reaches
with its sharp talons.
It catches the mouse.

3

An owl's eyes do not
move. So, the owl lowers its
neck to see what it is. It's a mouse!

YOUR NEW WORDS

anableps (**an**-uh-bleps) a fish that lives in the rivers of Mexico and South America

cricket (**krik**-it) a jumping insect

owl (oul) a bird with a round head, large eyes, and a head that spins; its head does not spin all the way around

scallop (**skal**-uhp) a shellfish with two shells

skull (skuhl) the bony part of the head

socket (**sok**-it) a hole or hollow place where something fits

spider (**spy**-dur) a small animal with eight legs

THESE ANIMALS HAVE AMAZING EYES, TOO!

bald eagle

tree frog

jaguar

sea lion

INDEX

FIND OUT MORE

Book:
Eyes by Elizabeth Miles, Heinemann Library, 2003

Website:
San Diego Natural History Museum
http://www.sdnhm.org/kids/eyes/sites.html

MEET THE AUTHOR:
Susan Labella is a freelance writer of books, articles, and magazines for kids. She is the author of other books in the *Scholastic News Nonfiction Readers* series. She lives in Connecticut and uses her eyes to help her write books for children like you!